The Disruptor's Guide to Avoiding Disruption

THE DISRUPTOR'S GUIDE TO AVOIDING DISRUPTION

All marketing and publishing rights guaranteed to and reserved by
Matthew J. Ratz
Email: mjratz@gmail.com
www.mattratz.org

Cover, text, and illustration design: Matthew Ratz

ISBN 13: 978-0-9836868-8-0

The Disruptor's Guide to Avoiding Disruption

Engaging, understanding, and preserving Millennial talent to improve 21ˢᵗ-Century workplaces

Text and Illustrations by Matthew Ratz

Disruptor:

A professional who—through his or her thoughts and actions—endeavors to "shake up" processes and unsettle environments to affect meaningful and positive change.

Table of Contents

Introduction

For all of my professional life, I have been a "disruptor." I didn't always know this, but it quickly became evident to me. In 2007, I was beginning my second year teaching at a Montgomery County, MD public high school. I had entered the teaching professional because my own student experience was a miserable one, and I was invigorated by the opportunity to break the cycle for my students by giving them a positive, uplifting, and energizing experience. My first year was a rousing success. My students left my classes feeling informed, engaged, and enlightened; the comments from their end-of-year feedback letters were all positive and encouraging toward my demeanor and my teaching methods.

Based upon this success, I was shifted from teaching "honors" classes to teaching "on-level" classes. When I was in school, I was in an "on-level" class, so I knew what the population was made of. The majority of my students in these classes—the vast majority that was not diagnosed with some formal learning disability—was made of bright kids who were discouraged from caring about school; this discouragement came primarily from teachers who couldn't connect content to students' interests.

Our first semester's experience reading Camus's *The Stranger* and studying existentialism was, for many of these students, the first time they read a book from cover to cover. We took 15 weeks to cover the novella, its philosophy, and that philosophy's overarching ramifications; we engaged in deep and provocative conversations that uplifted us all. At my semi-annual review with my administrator, I was asked if I was giving the students weekly worksheets on spelling and grammar. I replied that I was not. My administrator replied, "These kids' major issues are with spelling and grammar. They need worksheets to practice these skills. A good teacher understands that worksheets are the best tool for this practice."

I looked askance at this administrator, who had taught honors Latin for the past 12 years before becoming an Assistant Principal, and said, "Students do *not* need worksheets. In fact, worksheets are the least engaging tool to use. Over the past semester, my students have been actively participating in deep and thoughtful conversations about life; they've been engaged like never before. If giving students worksheets is the only way to be a 'good teacher,' then maybe I don't want to be one."

And with that I left the stable, decent-paying career as a public school teacher. I knew there was more to the world and more to life than fitting in to someone else's mold of a "good" professional.

Since that time, I have been on a one-man crusade to prove that life can be well-lived by one's own compass. This motto is the pulse of my generation.

Part I— Millennials' Backgrounds

Pop Quiz: Who said this?

"The children now love luxury; they have bad manners, contempt for authority; they show disrespect for elders and love chatter in place of discipline. Children ...no longer rise when elders enter the room. They contradict their parents, gossip before company... and tyrannize their teachers."

      (A)   Abraham Lincoln
      (B)   Joel Stein
      (C)   William Shakespeare
      (D)   Socrates

The answer is (D). That's right; according to Bartleby's, a web-based database of quotations, this statement has been attributed to Socrates. If he did, in fact, say this, it indicates that for 2,500 years, elders have been criticizing the behaviors and attitudes of their juniors. It can be argued that every generation, throughout history, has been critical and disparaging of its successive age group.

The fact remains, however, that each emerging generation—from "The Greatest Generation" from WWII to the Baby Boomers to Generation X—has caused tremendous disruption and necessitated the revamping of social and economic systems.

For instance:
- The women of the WWII generation paved the way for working mothers that persists to today.
- The Baby Boomers necessitated a shift to a new economic model and practiced stick-to-it-iveness and perseverance during social and economic turmoil.
- Generation X, with their technical abilities and independence, created the dot-com boom and established E-commerce as a major way of doing business.

The organizations who can harness the talents of the emerging professionals can position themselves for success in both the short-term and the long-term.

Managers and business owners in the current decade face a new crop of professionals who are emerging onto the world landscape: Millennials. Now, before you suggest that Millennials are no different than any previous generation— how they just represent every young worker population from time immemorial—check out these facts...

Realities for Millennials (born between 1982 and 2004):

- Personal computers have been a facet of everyday life since members of this generation were kids; IBM produced its last typewriter in 1990 when these folks were 7 or 8 years old.
- Throughout their lives, personal technology has been readily available to complete both simple— like phonebook and calendar—and complex—like project management and web design—tasks
- The costs of college, when combined with its necessity, have become outrageous and result in an average student loan debt that is nearly 300% larger than it was in 2006.
    - NBC News estimates the average class of 2011 debt at $26,600
- As their parents age and *don't* retire, Millennials become increasingly aware of "the myth of retirement" for their own generation; additionally, as Washington politicians continuously point to the unsustainability of Social Security and Medicare, Millennials see any "safety net" evaporating before their times come.
- The majority of students who earned degrees in the last five years have been faced with the toughest job market in memory
    - A Rutgers University survey conducted of grads from 2006-2011 indicate that only 50% of graduates from this date range are working full-time

As a result of these experiences from their earliest childhood memories to their recent completion of a staggeringly-expensive and cost-*in*effective college education, Millennials have shaped their own, unique Millennial Personality

As a member of this generation, I fall in line with this biography. Additionally, my employment history demonstrates the effects of these upbringing idiosyncrasies.

For instance, I have had a PC in my home since I was 12; I have handled each technological advancement from Teddy Ruxpin to Tomagochi to Palm Pilots to iPhones. Though I was able to afford college on my parents' backs with minimal loans, I still owe over $25,000 in loans for undergrad and grad school. (This, despite my having earned *less* in every starting salary since I finished my Master's in 2006). Also, although my parents are nearing retirement age, neither of them has enough stashed away to even imagine retiring before age 70+. (My in-laws, who have retired, still maintain part-time jobs, not because they *want* to.) Personally, since grad school, I have held no less than seven full- and part-time jobs. Despite there being many counterexamples among my peers, I believe my situation is typical of the average Millennial. Here's why...

As a group, Millennials...
- recognize, from their parents' layoffs and financial struggles, that loyalty to one company throughout one's career is *not* a wise investment of time or energy

- often feel talked down to or slighted, even as they are deemed the "most educated" generation of all time; any conversation on the contrast between "educated" and "smart," when initiated by elders, seems patronizing and pedantic
- tend to prefer work that makes an impact—whether real or perceived; a paycheck is often not enough of a motivator for them to persist in a challenging but unrewarding job
- view the concept of "paying your dues" as both repugnant and unrewarding

The challenge to managers: How do you harness the positive qualities of this generation to improve your businesses and our society?

Part II—Outline

You may ask, "What are the positive qualities of this age group? Aren't they just *entitled*, *haughty*, and *lazy?*" While I haven't been called those things to my face, I imagine some managers have felt that way.

Realize that your preceding generation most likely believed the same about you, but the lack of world-wide communication and a certain degree of professional etiquette, ensured that you would never know it.

Millennials, as a generation, are perceived to have the following challenges:

- they need "trophies" for minor accomplishments;
- they seek constant, immediate, and ever-positive feedback;
- they are focused on themselves, almost narcissistically;
- they never put down their smartphones or tablets;

On the flip-side, Millennials typically have some of the following strengths—

- Social Media Savvy
- Informal Communications Skills
- Intrinsic Motivation to Give Back
- Technical Skill
- A Wellspring of Ideas
- Strong Customer Focus
- Blending the Personal and Professional

Which of those strengths does *not* translate into greater innovation, new leads, increased customer satisfaction and retention, and overall corporate success, both social and financial? The key is to leverage or harness these strengths without coming off as inauthentic or disingenuous; by and large, Millennials have a great "B.S. sensor" and are acutely aware when someone is trying to manipulate them.

The challenge, then, is to develop authentic processes and leverage true-to-self management tools to empower Millennial workers and synergistically improve their performance and the company's bottom-line concurrently.

Bull Detector

Objectives

What we will examine through this work will be three-fold:

1. We're going to examine how the particular strengths of a Millennial worker can yield profits—both social and economic.

2. We're going to break down some management myths whose practice and long-term implications stymie Millennial workers' creativity as well as their impact.

3. We're going to develop new tools—based on best practices in the field of Education—to empower, coach, and improve Millennials' performances so they are positioned to actualize the changes they imagine.

Part III—Millennials' Strengths

Let's start by examining the strengths Millennials bring to the current and future employers. For each identified strength, we can explore avenues how this skill-set is profit-producing.

#1. Millennials are constantly "plugged-in"; they are checking Facebook and Twitter continuously; they are viewing media on the go; they are communicating at lightning speed with their peers.

There is no easier way to be on the cutting edge of a specialty than by being connected. The challenge for managers is to foster meaningful connectivity by pointing Millennials to the right sources. For example, there are industry-specific Twitter feeds that share best practices and new insights. There are particular professionals on Facebook and LinkedIn who share insights and innovative ideas. By channeling Millennials' technological skills, businesses can innovate and pivot more easily.

#2. Millennials are used to the education system after 16+ years of formal schooling. They might not appreciate hierarchies or protocols, but they understand that content-matter expertise and authenticity are highly valued commodities.

Millennials recognize when someone is passionate and knowledgeable; at the same time, Millennials can quickly detect "BS". This can be leveraged—especially on sales teams or with client services—to determine if a client is "just playing hardball" or is uniquely disinterested. These skills can save valuable time and energy to focus on prospects that are worth the chase.

#3. Millennials are comfortable merging the professional and the personal. This sometimes means having friendships with coworkers that are maintained after working hours, but this can also mean building a solid customer base out of existing friends.

This is a generation that grew up selling raffle tickets, Girl Scout cookies, and relay-race laps to their families and neighbors; this skill-set can be a boon for a business that needs to generate new leads and build-up test markets.

#4. Millennials are innovative, and not penned in by "that's just the way it is" mentalities.

A Millennial will be wired to view a situation from a unique angle, one that is typically ignored by older colleagues. A Millennial worker is more likely to employ an outlandish strategy, yet one that can completely

14

revolutionize organizational problem solving. This new perspective and this "unbound" thinking style is uniquely well-suited to tough problems or when drastic changes are necessary.

Of course, these are just a few of Millennials' many strengths. With a careful and creative eye toward leveraging skills, businesses can find a way to maximize returns on the natural acumen of this generation.

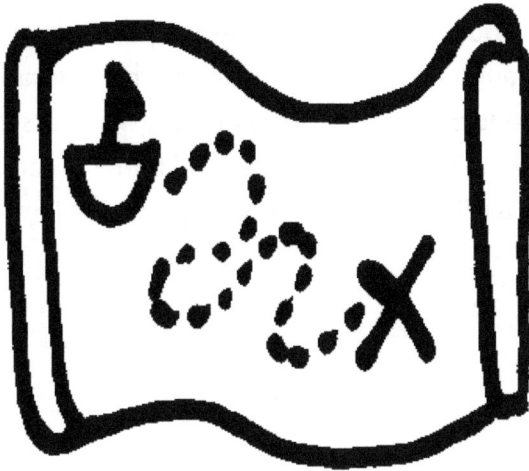

Charting a New Course

Part IV—Management Gaffes

There are several "management techniques" that have been floating around since the stone-age that really undermine a manager's abilities to leverage Millennials' talents. Most modern management techniques are based, in some way, in motivation theory *a la* Abraham Maslow or his contemporaries; some other tools emerge from schools of communication and the expressive-receptive language dichotomy. In the end, any tool that is authentic and emerges out of a manager's personality can be useful in maximizing the returns from his or her employees; however, inauthentic or poorly-leveraged techniques will backfire, especially with Millennials who are highly sensitive to fakeness.

There are three tools or approaches that are uniquely unproductive for Millennial employees. These are: (1) the praise-critique-praise "feedback sandwich" (2) Brainstorms, and (3) the "Four P's." Each of these is replaced by a more-appropriate augmentation that takes into consideration Millennials' educations and levels of self-awareness. First we can examine the three approaches, and then we can contrast them to more effective tools for managers of Millennials.

#1. The "Feedback Sandwich"

For decades, managers (or anyone giving feedback) has been advised to provide feedback with a P-C-P structure. First, praise some quality or trait, then critique the specific behavior, and then end with a general praising statement of ability or strength. This approach has become so ubiquitous that when praise is offered in a workplace, employees start guessing what will follow the "but."

This both minimizes the quality of the praise and diminishes the clarity of the critique. An employee may think, "If I'm a strong contributor to the team, then why should my numbers be criticized?"

A better approach is two-fold. Managers need to praise publicly without hesitation, so if an employee is observed doing the right thing, praise on the spot. At the same time, criticism must be given privately, and must be focused on concrete behaviors and solutions, not on abstract attitudes and problems. For example, if an employee has an attendance problem, which would be a better approach?

(A) You're always late to work, and this makes you look unprofessional and reckless. You'll never be successful here if you can't get to work on time! If you come late one more time, there will be dire consequences.

Or...

(B) When you arrive to work late, I perceive that you are not serious about your work; if I have this feeling, I imagine our clients do too, and this causes us—and you, by extension—to lose revenue and opportunities. I believe you care about your work, so please show it by arriving on time.

Approach A places the blame on the employee's attitude and the manager's perception of it. It also sets up a threat—both real ("dire consequences") and perceived ("never be successful here"). Furthermore, it uses a tremendous amount of "you" language and loaded, universalizing phrases. When a person is confronted with "you" accusations like, "You're *always*…" one cannot help but become defensive.

Approach B, on the other hand, sets up the relationship between the employee's behavior and the manager's and the customers' perceptions of it; it also provides a choice for the employee ("I know you care…please show it") and uses "I" language ("I perceive…I imagine…I believe"). "I" language diffuses conflict and sounds much less accusatory; it can be taken less offensively and typically leads to more positive results and rapport.

Both qualify as critiques, but the second is much more likely to yield a behavioral change because it couches the behavior in a real consequence—the loss of revenue due to perceived unprofessionalism and does not sound like an indictment; plus, it does not state that this is a universal behavior (i.e. *always* happening), so it creates a space for change.

#2. Brainstorms

For many years, the best approach to solving a problem has been the "brainstorming" meeting. This meeting, characterized by the "free flow of ideas," has been a staple of businesses. What typically happens during a brainstorming meeting is this: the leader presents a quandary and opens the floor to suggestions. Then, typically, an energetic scribe will scribble ideas onto whiteboards and wall-sized sticky notes until everyone's spoken his or her piece. What emerges, most often, is a wealth of half-baked and well-intentioned ideas that no one on the team actually wants to implement. Yet, the invitation to "speak freely" inspires nearly-useless solutions.

Studies have shown that better ideas emerge when two conditions are met: (1) Individuals who share ideas have a "devil's advocate" to offer potential pitfalls and (2) Individuals are held accountable for actualizing their ideas. Neither of these are born in a brainstorming session. Instead, employees should be given constructive criticism on the spot (not destructive criticism like "that'll never work!" but constructive questions like "what if this happens...?") and they should be asked, once a solution is presented, if they would head up the task-force to implement the solution. Suddenly, a wall-splash of ideas turns into two or three really thought-through ideas and in-born team leaders willing to shepherd them.

#3. The "Four P's"

Since Business Marketing has been a formal school of thought, so for nearly a century, its "Four P's" have been central. Product, Price, Place, and Promotion are typically the first thoughts that come to anyone introducing a new product or service into the market. However, new considerations have to be factored into customers' (or even employees') decision-making calculus. New requirements like Processes, People, and physical Evidence are now factored into decision making.

And though the Four P's have been an element of marketing for many years, they have also become an element of hiring and on-boarding processes. Millennials care about the Products they represent, the location, or Place, of their employment; they also care about the Price, or salary, and the Promotion, or fringe benefits that will come along with employment. But, Millennials will also be clued in to the People with whom they work—are they smart, capable, energized; the Processes of the workplace—whether they are efficient and ethical—as well as Physical Evidence of a positive work environment and positive impact such as colleagues who smile, an inviting atmosphere, and testimonials from clients and customers.

Managers and employers must consider how a workplace is marketed to future employees, especially Millennial workers. Because of the new P's of People, Processes, and Physical Evidence, Millennial employees will scour the Web for clues, feedback, and current- and prior-employee testimonials before agreeing to sign-on with an organization. Though the economy may wax and wane, Millennials' internal needs to make an impact will draw them to ethical and authentic organizations time after time.

The Platinum Rule

Before we continue, I want to address a famous piece of advice from Tony Alessandra often called "The Platinum Rule." Most of us have been familiar with "the golden rule": treat others how you would like to be treated. Alessandra explains that the golden rule doesn't work as well as his "platinum rule" to treat others the way *they* want to be treated, or, as he puts it, "Do unto others as they would like to be done unto." For inter-generational relationships between a Baby Boomer manager and a Millennial employee, the only way to exercise the platinum rule is to engage in meaningful dialogue around wants and needs from both groups. Though a Millennial may not be as articulate in expressing his or her motivations, having engaged in the conversation to discern how he or she would like to be treated will give traction to future interactions.

Additionally, as for most employees, engaging Millennials in conversations about how they would like to receive feedback and performance evaluations, and holding them accountable for their responses by acting upon them will build a positive relationship between a manager and his Millennial employees.

Part V—A Better Approach

Five decades ago, the management guru Peter Drucker initiated the concept of management by objectives. This educational approach measures an employee's performance alongside his or her awareness of and fidelity to pre-stated objectives. This style requires several preliminary steps. First, a manager needs to have a clear sense of the employee's purpose or role. Second, the processes to be used must be easily spelled out. Third, both the employee and his or her manager need to agree on both the demarcated roles and the processes. And finally, an employee must be held accountable for his or her achievement of the pre-stated goals using a valid and transparent performance-measurement tool.

In a labor economy—one in which a person's product is a measure of his skill—this may not have been necessary. And Drucker, being perpetually ahead of the curve, recognized the shift from a labor industry to a knowledge industry years before anyone else (in fact, he coined the term "Knowledge Worker"). This management-by-objective (MBO) strategy became a mainstay of the modern managerial toolkit; however, its underlying concept can be upended by the Millennials' arrivals, unless it is tweaked.

Why is management by objective, in its current form, ineffective for Millennial workers? Well, let's examine the preliminary steps. Typically, when a Millennial is hired, he or she is aware that an entry-level position is a stepping stone on to something larger. If a manager's concept of a professional's role is fixed and stagnant, this will immediately sour the employee-manager dynamic and discourage an employee's best work. Millennials want to know that there is an upward trend to their employment, so non-evolving roles become frustrating.

Additionally, it is rare, in this ever-changing landscape that is the professional world, that a singular process will be clear and routine; more often, a professional needs to experiment, morph, and augment processes in order to achieve greater results. If processes are frozen, true innovation cannot occur. Finally, because Millennials tend to be dismissive or oppositional to hierarchical relationships, solid-line supervisory tactics can backfire or feel too much like micromanagement to a Millennial employee.

For Management by Objectives to work, a supervisor starts the process by painting a picture of the completed project. "What will it accomplish?" and "Whom will it benefit?" are the key concerns. What the finished item looks like, sounds like, or moves like is not as much of a concern. The advice for managers who want to foster independence is to focus not on methodologies but on outcomes instead.

For example, in a non-profit sector, if the outcome is that 50% more of the population of underprivileged students have access to nutritious meals during school, the manager cannot be concerned if the nutrition comes in the form of regular snacks or protein shakes or deli sandwiches; nor should the manager be worried about the workload demands of lunch servers or the interruption of classroom instruction. If the outcome is more students have food, then that is what should be measured; the product, not the process. MBO tends to be a better tool for Millennials because it unties the reins and allows creativity and a new perspective to rule the day. It has been said, if one wants to foster independence in his employees, he must focus on results, not on methods; like I stated above, this is the enhancement to Drucker's Management by Objectives.

Part VI—A New-ish Model

For decades, now, an educational "best practice" has been energizing classrooms around the world. Though it is sometimes called different things, "Differentiation" seems to be the nomenclature to describe this instructional revolution. Differentiation, instead of focusing on the interests and skills of the instructor, looks instead to the interests, talents, and needs of the learner to drive instruction. This approach has been "all the rage" sine the 1990s, and continues to be a fierce opponent of the standardized testing culture most schools have regressed toward.

Millennials most likely had some experience, throughout their long academic careers, with some element of differentiation; whether this included some choice when completing assessments, or project-based learning, or even a "flipped classroom" approach, Millennials are used to their teachers making efforts to connect content to their levels of interest and need. Say what you will about this approach, but having taught middle school students, high school students, college-aged students, and adults, I can attest to the engaging and empowering force of differentiation and leveraging student choice in the instructional setting.

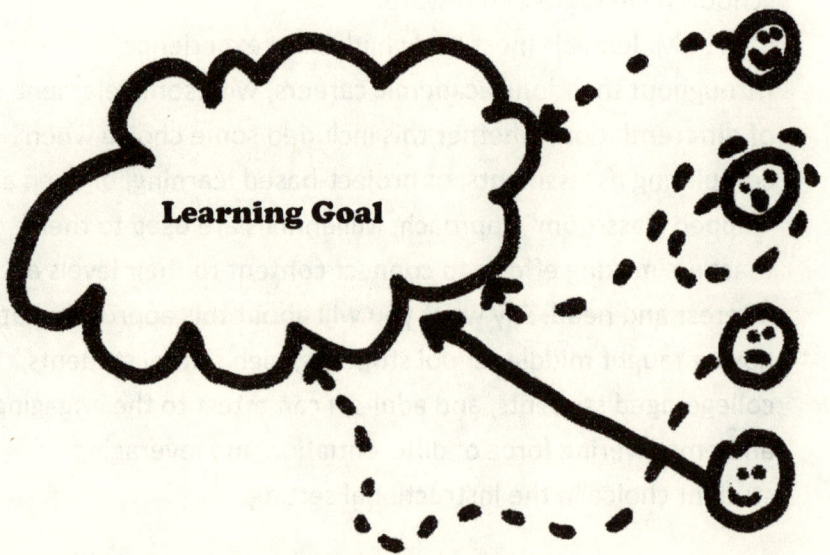

Learning Goal

How can managers of for-profit and non-profit companies use this tool? How does a fringe educational approach have any effect on the corporate landscape? Well, surprisingly, how students get used to learning in school has a large impact on their openness to and ability to digest instructions throughout their lives. And since Millennials are the "most educated" generation, taking a page from their teachers' manuals may not be a bad way to engage, empower, and enhance what they bring to our organizations.

Differentiation, broadly defined, is when an educator responds to the learners' needs and is guided by his or her mindset (i.e. the belief that students can or cannot build new skills) to flex the content, process, or expected product within the learning environment. In layman's terms, differentiation means understanding that all students will not learn in the same ways, and not all students will be able to demonstrate what they've learned in the same ways.

The differentiated model can be applied quite easily to the workplace and leveraged to enable Millennials (and their managers) to experience quick and long-lasting success in their professional roles. Differentiation can be applied to (a) the screening of application materials, it can be applied to (b) new-hiring training and probationary periods, and it can be applied to (c) regular evaluations to retain key talent. Each of these settings will be further explored through the next section.

Differentiating Applicants

Many Human Resources departments operate on the axiom, "Past performance predicts future performance" (the acronym 3P.F.P.). As a result of this statement—which is, in many cases, true as the sunrise—recruitment procedures emerge that assess past performance; the resume and cover letter listing employment chronologies and career highlights exist to discern how the applicant views his or her success in past endeavors. Letters of recommendation or a reference list can serve to discern how applicants' former managers and colleagues perceived his or her success in past endeavors. A criminal background check can discern if applicants have violated laws and policies in the past. All of these are measures that typically clarify past performance and can, with some degree of efficiency, help to deduce if someone will be successful in a similar occupation.

But, there are a few things wrong with the current cycle of resume + cover letter + references + background check. The first issue is that most of these documents are controlled by the applicant. A savvy job searcher knows how to tweak and wordsmith documents and how to select references with alacrity so that their records glow. These same savvy searchers have learned to downplay past failures and interview with a fluency that makes them irresistible job applicants.

At the same time, the 3P.F.P acronym works well to predict how one will do in a similar job, but what about a career changer or a "renaissance person" whose true talents lay outside his or her professional roles? Can a resume of past jobs and managers' recommendations serve to recommend a person switching from data entry to broadcast journalism? Can talents be revealed for someone moving from hairdressing to social-media management? The current application material cache pigeonholes job seekers and it pigeonholes recruiters, too. If we are trained only to look for what is black-and-white before us, we neglect to see what is on the periphery; we neglect to imagine what's possible. You'll recall that a talent of Millennials is the ability to approach problems in new ways; however, if the job-search process is trapped in a world of "only seeing what's directly in front of us," Millennials may never be given the chance to shake things up for the better.

Best Practices in Applicant Screening

The task for recruiters and hiring managers, then, is to devise a way to assess applicants' *potential* instead of past performance. The interview process is typically billed as "finding the best person for the job," but those invited to interview are those who composed the best admission tickets. How, then, can we differentiate this process to attract and hire truly the best and brightest?

A "best practice" in client screening is a behavioral-based interview which focuses on solving realistic problems. Instead of an interviewer asking the applicant, "Tell me about yourself," one might ask, "In this role, you'll be faced with disciplining subordinates while maintaining meaningful relationships with them; tell me about a time when you did something similar, but maintained camaraderie." Instead of the question, "What is your best quality and what is your worst quality?" an interviewer can ask, "Your resume indicates strength in strategic planning, what would you propose the first step should be as we sharpen our business' mission statement?" By couching questions in the behavioral-based response to real-world problems, interviewers using behavioral questioning are better able to tell who has the "chops" to deal with organization's real issues.

Another "best practice," this time among job seekers, is the development of a living portfolio that accompanies a resume and cover letter. Through this dynamic collection of physical evidence, truly capable applicants can showcase their achievements both within and outside of the professional landscape. Once the domain of visual artists or performance professionals, portfolios are quickly becoming a go-to tool for businesspeople, financial planners, educators, and consultants; these web-based or paper-based documentaries of skill help separate the "wheat from the chaff" in an interview environment.

When I was interviewing for my first teaching position in 2006 (and my three subsequent teaching positions in 2009, 2010, and 2012), I always brought an updated portfolio of students' and parents' feedback, classroom assessments, photographs, lesson plans, and educational philosophies. Of the 15 interviews I have been on for teaching positions, only two even glanced at my portfolio; none giving it the attention and time it merited. An elongated glance at my portfolio would have revealed my classroom management philosophy, my assessment style, and my rapport with students; understanding these three areas could have been immeasurably valuable to those who wanted to manage me administratively. This represents a failed opportunity for past managers.

If employers are serious about employing "the best," time needs to be set aside for assessing these applicants at appropriate lengths that realistically measure their aptitude and their potential. This is especially true given the spotted work histories of Millennials, and even truer given Millennials' mindsets about the triviality of loyalty to an employer. If a position is just a stepping stone and a Millennial senses that his or her true worth is being undervalued or misjudged, even if he is the best one for the job, the job will not be the best fit for him and a truly powerful opportunity will be squandered.

Differentiating Trainings

One of the keys for differentiating instruction is assessing prior knowledge. Through surveys, presentations, or written work, teachers are able to discern what students *already* know; through these methods teachers can save time by quickly reviewing areas of strength and focusing, instead, on misconceptions or areas of need.

Think how useful this system could be for training and on-boarding new hires to an organization! I recall, when I was being "on-boarded" to my many different organizations, each had its own approach. Before beginning my year teaching inner-city students, my school took all of its teachers on a weekend retreat where we collaboratively developed policies and procedures we all could agree with. On the flipside, when I began my professorship at a two-year college, I had two hours of on-boarding followed by a series of optional and oddly-timed sessions (none of which I was able to attend due to other obligations). In my current role, I had an entire month of on-boarding training prior to my being able to begin my actual work.

Each organization has its priorities; some are really keen on a collaborative culture, others are concerned about uniform processes, and still others are concerned with creative problem-solving. Some companies care that employees all know their mission statements while others care that the company's history be taught. Whatever the priority, though, some employees will come to on-boarding with more background knowledge than others. These employees deserve the respect for their background knowledge and do not need to be subjugated to tiresome trainings that are redundant.

What is incumbent upon training departments, then, is to devise a meaningful assessment of prior knowledge. Perhaps, if a company prioritizes project management, aligning processes to the PMP® assessment and requiring that designation for employees is a better way to on-board than to spend weeks training *everyone* on project-management processes. Maybe, if organizational history is important, a pencil-and-paper assessment can be delivered to see what new employees already know about the company before entering a three-hour history lesson on its founders' principles. Much time and capital can be saved by strategically tailoring a training schedule for each new employee that avoids redundancies while assessing prior knowledge. I know, for instance, that I could have been 100% more productive during my first month on the job had I been allowed to "hit the ground running" instead of sitting in a month of trainings that were redundant based on my experience and education.

Differentiating Evaluations

Another of the core tenets of differentiation is the idea that no learner will be able to demonstrate mastered knowledge in quite the same way as his or her peers. Despite this, most organizations use the same tool—be it a grid, a rubric, or a written performance review—to assess their professionals' growth, strengths, and weaknesses.

I recall, when I first stumbled upon the idea of differentiated assessment, my peers who were more-veteran teachers said, "Wow. That'll be a ton of work." Now, they were 100% correct, designing assessments to enable students to genuinely demonstrate their mastery *was* a ton of work; yet, the results far outweighed the time it took to design these assessment tools. I could say with complete confidence what each student did and did not take away from my instruction; I could tailor my instruction more effectively; I could add lessons where necessary and redact others that were redundant.

Wouldn't it be of great benefit for managers to have a variety of measurement tools by which an employee's true strengths and weaknesses can be assessed? Though this may be difficult at first, if the goal of employment is steady and consistent growth, then meaningful assessment is the linchpin for achieving this goal. Employee evaluations can come in the form of written evaluations, self-completed surveys, portfolios, documentary evidence (films and photographs), interviews, or any other method that will accurately uncover accomplishments and areas of continued need.

Like asking employees how they would prefer to receive feedback, soliciting their opinions about how they would like their progress to be measured may be a challenging discussion at first, but it will add immeasurably to an employee's ability to submit to said evaluation because he or she will have had a hand in crafting how the assessment is done.

Summing it All Up

A 2009 article by a professor of Chinese language works to debunk the famous self-help phrase that crisis is danger plus opportunity. The idea comes from a statement often attributed to John F. Kennedy about how the Chinese symbol for "crisis" (*weiji*) is made up of the logographs for "danger" (*wei*) and for "opportunity" (*ji*). The fact that this is a misnomer, as the author takes strides to prove, serves only to demonstrate the phrase's utility in the area of self-help. Many prefer the Pollyannaish notion of "crisis= danger + opportunity." It is from that paradigm that I wrap up.

As we've explored, the Millennial generation comes to the workplace with a lot of baggage. They come both with promise and potential as well as with contempt and over-confidence. The opportunities presented to managers in this day and age are unprecedented throughout History; there is more potential for meaningful change among members of the Millennial generation than in any previous generation. Businesses and organizations would do well to tap this resource.

Of course, tapping a valuable resource brings as much trouble as return-on-investment. If companies want to be able to truly maximize the opportunities presented by Millennials, they will need to adjust how and why they do business. Through recognizing individuals' capabilities while concurrently differentiating processes across the employment lifespan, managers and corporations can actualize the promise presented by the Millennials, a generation of eager, well-educated, and entrepreneurial individuals.

www.ingramcontent.com/pod-product-compliance
Lightning Source LLC
LaVergne TN
LVHW041210080426
835508LV00008B/885